Success...an adventure

Learning to think for yourself and to work with others

Alejandrina Gonzalez
Danilo Sirias, Ph.D.
Aurora Guerra
Marina Rodríguez
Evangelina Salazar

If you wish to receive further information about the thinking tools presented in this book and their application to education please address all correspondence to

Danilo Sirias, Ph.D.
7400 Bay Road
University Center, MI 48710
USA
e-mail: dsirias@svsu.edu

For additional copies of this book visit:

www.lulu.com/DSirias

Acknowledgments

The thinking tools presented in this book are part of the body of knowledge referred to as the Theory of Constraints and were developed by Dr. Eli Goldratt. We want to thank him for creating and donating this valuable knowledge to schools all over the world.

We would like to thank all the people who helped us make this book possible.

Success... an adventure

Saturday the 4th
8:00 PM

"Dinner time!" George hears his mom calling.

George is a good-looking, 16-year-old boy. He is the tallest boy in the school and has light brown hair and a profound look of happiness in his eyes. His best feature, however, is his big smile. George is a party and sports lover. He is the dream guy for girls, an active reader, and usually a good decision maker.

George is in ninth grade and lately his grades have fallen. His parents are constantly arguing with him that his grades would improve if only he got more sleep.

George has changed a lot. Before, he could fix everything just by asking for his parents' help. But now he is mature enough to make his own decisions, which is not easy. He feels his parents don't understand him. They believe he is a trouble-maker, and this annoys him. Don't they realize that there are situations where these problems come on their own?

He has many new friends, both boys and girls. In the beginning, having so many different friends wasn't easy, but with time they got to know each other better and have strengthened their friendships. They have shared the good times and the bad. The girls have learned to enjoy soccer games, and the boys find it entertaining to join girls on their shopping marathons. Although they have differences regarding gender and particular interests, they have found great fun in sharing these moments.

Five minutes later... "Dinner's ready!" his mom yells again.

George opens his bedroom door and answers with a very angry tone, "I'm not having dinner. I'm busy!"

Louise is a very traditional and family-oriented mother. She is very devoted to her family, and she's always gotten along well with her two sons, Al and George. But since George started high school, the relationship between them has changed. They argue constantly, and what used to be a peaceful and happy home is now a battlefield. The missiles are thrown from all directions. At any given time, you can't tell who the enemies are.

Louise goes to George's room and knocks on the door. "What's the matter George?" Louise asks as she enters the room.

George answers in an angry tone, "What do you want? I'm on the phone! I already told you that I was busy."

Louise angrily replies, "This is out of line. You will never talk to me that way again!"

Louise retreats to the kitchen asking herself, "In what moment did the communication I had with George get so bad? What must he be thinking to be acting like that? He is so irritable. He gets angry about everything. He won't talk to me anymore, and whenever I ask him what is wrong, he answers very angrily, 'I'm okay. Leave me alone. I know exactly what I'm doing.'"

George's father, Frank, is sitting in his favorite chair at the dinner table. He lights another cigarette as he waits for

George and Louise. His other son, Al, is not having dinner with them. Frank sees Louise approaching. George isn't with her.

"I heard you talking with George," Frank tells Louise. "What happened? Was he being disrespectful again?"

"No... well... at the beginning... but," answers Louise, trying to justify George.

"No! Even the neighbors could hear you. Are you protecting him again?" Frank asks as his voice rises.

"Let's eat," Louise says as she tries to change the conversation. "We are having dinner alone."

8:30 PM

"You're not going to the party, and that's final!" Frank screamed at George.

"That's totally unfair. I can't cancel on Lucy. It's her birthday party. I promised!" George yelled back.

"Too bad! I refuse to be spoken to in that tone!" Frank yelled. He was breathless and was clutching at his chest.

"I'm going and you can't stop me!" George yelled as he left the room. Frank was holding on to the banister. He started coughing. Sweat was rolling down his face. He started to feel lightheaded. Frank headed up the stairs.

"Louise!" he yelled, gasping for breath.

"Yes," she said as she entered the room.

"I'm not feeling too well," he said. George came into the room again. At the same moment, Frank fell backwards. Time slowed for George as his father keeled backwards down the stairs. Every step Frank hit sounded like a muffled thump to George. Frank landed on the floor and rolled over, unconscious. Louise ran over to Frank.

"Frank!" she cried. From the top of the stairs came Al's voice.

"Mom, what happened?" he said, rushing down the stairs.

"Al, call 911," Louise said. Al rushed to the phone and dialed. George was as still as a statue. He felt as if his feet were glued to the ground. He stared at his father lying on the ground, pale and covered in sweat.

Monday the 6th
7:50AM

"Teacher! Miss Patty!" yells George.

Miss Patty is George's homeroom teacher. She is short and plump and wears comfortable, fashionable clothes. Miss Patty is always looking for new educational techniques to improve her impact on her students. Even though she is young, she has had great experience working with teenagers. Her kindness and humanity helped her to gain trust and respect not only from her students, but also from her colleagues. Parents like to talk with her, and they really listen to her good advice.

"What's wrong George? Why are you so angry?" asks Miss Patty patiently.

"I can't stand my parents anymore!" George desperately yells.

"Miss Patty," George insists. "I've been explaining to my parents that I can only have fun at parties for a few years, and they don't understand. Now my dad is in the hospital because of me. I can't believe it."

"Hospital…why? What happened?" asks Miss Patty in a worried tone.

"We were arguing and suddenly he fainted. He rolled down the stairs and we had to take him to the hospital," explains George.

"How is he now?" asks Miss Patty.

"He doesn't look very good. The doctors are running some tests, and they haven't said anything yet. Now I feel horrible for arguing with him, but the truth is that we're always arguing," says George.

"Why do you think you can never talk with him and that you always end up arguing?" asks Miss Patty.

"Well, I don't really know, but we always end up in a fight. We never stop arguing," said George. "They don't understand me anymore. I'm always wrong and everything is always my fault. Sometimes I'm a child to them, and sometimes I'm an adult to them. I don't get them."

"I want to go to Lucy's party. I don't want to disappoint her; it is her birthday party," says George.

"Why did you argue this time with your dad? Can you explain it in a calm way?" asks Miss Patty.

"Well, I think you are asking too much. I don't know if I can explain it in a calm way," says George.

"We'll see. Tell me exactly what your problem is," says Miss Patty.

"Are you serious? You don't know what my problem is? I want to go to Lucy's party, and my dad won't let me!" George yells.

"If you keep yelling like that, everyone in this school will think there's something seriously wrong," says Miss Patty.

"Sorry, I'm just furious. And when I think about it, I get even angrier. It's impossible for my dad and me to reach an agreement. I won't give in, and neither will he. We're both angry and we can't find a solution. I don't think there is a solution," says George.

"Are you sure about that?" asks Miss Patty.

"Of course I am! Parents and teachers always win. They are the authority; so, they're always right and we're always wrong. I'm going to that party. That's a fact! But I'm worried about Dad's health. I don't know what might happen," says George, who is worried that everything he does makes things worse.

"If you say that parents are always right, do what you are told and then you won't have any problems. I don't see the problem," suggests Miss Patty.

George had zoned out. "What did you say? See, teachers and parents are always right. We are never going to win. I want to go to that party! That is important, too! Teenagers like me can decide, think, and act, too," says George.

"Is that what you think? That parents and teachers are always right? Do you think it can be different?" Miss Patty asks.

"Yes, of course it can be different. We can be right sometimes," says George.

"If you win and your parents lose, will you be happy?" asks Miss Patty.

"Of course I will," answers George.

"And then, will they be happy?" asks Miss Patty.

George is quiet for a few seconds. "It has always been that way, Miss Patty. If there's a winner, there's a loser too," George answers.

"Is that written somewhere?" asks Miss Patty.

George was silent. He is not used to so many questions about the way he thinks, and he wonders what Miss Patty is up to.

"You told me when you first came to this school that you were very happy, because your parents gave you the opportunity to choose where to study. You were going to prove to them that you were responsible for your own decision. Isn't that true?" asks Miss Patty.

"Yes, it's true," answers George.

"So, tell me now, who won that time?" continues Miss Patty.

"Well, I guess we both did," George says quietly. "Well, I think... the truth is I don't really know. I'm confused."

"I understand perfectly. When we have problems, we get so confused that we don't see clearly and we can't find solutions. It's as if a big cloud prevents us from seeing the light. The challenge is to find a solution where there are no losers. And, the important thing is to think reasonably and have the self-control to find the solution where both sides are winners."

"I'm going to show you something," Miss Patty says. She shows George a paper with a drawing on it. "What do you see?" asks Miss Patty.

"Let me see," George says as he looks at the paper. George stares at the paper for a few seconds. "Oh, I see. It's an Indian head carved in rock!"

"Are you sure that's the only thing you see?" asks Miss Patty.

"Yeah, I am not that blind," George replies.

"Are you sure? Look closely..." insists Miss Patty.

"Oh, I know. It's one of those tricky drawings! Give me a little more time. I know there should be another drawing," George says.

George continues to watch the drawing for a while and then says, "I can't see anything. Is there really anything else?"

"Yes, yes there is. I see the drawing," says Miss Patty.

The bell rings, announcing class.

The morning passes slowly. George has not been able to concentrate in class. Because of what's happening with his dad, he feels very tense.

2:00 PM

George leaves school without stopping to talk with his friends like he usually does. He heads down to the hospital to see his father's progress and to find out if they have any news from the doctors.

"George!" yells Ruben as he tries to reach him. "I bet you're going to the hospital. I'll come. We all talked during lunch, and we want to help you. Just tell me what you need."

Ruben is George's best friend, and they've been neighbors since they were kids. Ruben is not as tall as George. He has an athletic body and small green eyes. He has a great passion for all sports, but soccer is his favorite. He is captain of the soccer team. If somebody has a question about sports, all they have to do is ask Ruben. Even though he has many admirers, he is shy and reserved.

"Maggie sent you this note," Ruben tells George as they walk to the hospital. "You know how she is, always worrying about everyone."

As George opens the letter, he says, "Yeah, last night I saw her at the hospital. She was there visiting her uncle. She stayed with me for a while. Maggie is very cool. I never thought I could open up to a girl. I always thought they were too sensitive, especially Maggie, but talking with her was comforting. She was very supportive.

"You're lucky George! I wish I could talk like that with a girl someday," says Ruben.

At the hospital, George's mother is resting on the sofa. His father is sleeping soundly. Louise woke up when she felt the presence of George and Ruben. George asks Louise as he gives her a kiss on the forehead, "How is dad doing? Are the results back?"

"No, Champ. They're still not ready. We won't know until the doctor tells us. Nevertheless, I'm not worried, because he believes it's nothing serious. For the moment, they gave him a sedative and he'll be sleeping all afternoon."

"You can go home and rest for a while," George says to Louise. "I'm going to stay here all afternoon. I brought my books to do some homework."

"But you haven't eaten. I would feel better if you eat first," Louise replies.

"Sure, George. Let's go to the cafeteria and eat quickly so that your mom can go home soon," suggests Ruben.

4:30 PM

Al, George's older brother, arrives at the hospital, finds the boys studying, and greets them.

Ruben starts to pick up his stuff and says, "It's time for me to leave."

Al approaches his dad but realizes he is in a deep sleep. So, he decides to sit down on the futon next to George. "Any news?" he asks George.

George says, "Not yet. Tonight the doctor will tell us the results. But, mom says the doctor told her that it wasn't anything serious. That's why I asked her to go home and rest for a while."

"That's good! She must have been tired from spending the night on this horrible futon," says Al.

"Are you going back to work or are you free this afternoon?" asks George.

"No, I have everything arranged. I'm going to stay here," replies Al.

After a brief silence, George says to Al in a low voice, "I feel bad because of what happened. It's my fault dad got sick. We're always arguing."

"Don't beat yourself up. I've argued with him many times and never made him sick. I'm sure it's something else. You know how he smokes and never exercises."

"I hope so. I would never forgive myself if anything happened because of me," George slowly replies.

Tuesday the 7th
8:00 AM

The highly anticipated soccer match is finally here. Both high schools have trained hard, and they are both nervous because this game will decide the championship.

The game has been very close. Both teams have been giving all their effort. The crowd is euphoric.

"Goal!" screams the crowd. Luis celebrates his goal by running all over the field. At that moment, the referee blows his whistle. Everybody turns to see him.

"Offside!" yells the referee.

George's team goes to see the referee because they can't believe that he'd made such a bad call. The school cheerleaders, wanting to support their friends, increase the volume of their cheers.

"Offside! This is unbelievable! It was a goal. There's no doubt about it," yells the coach.

The game goes on with only three minutes left in the first half. The score is tied at 1-1. The cheers get louder. The girls join the cheers. Everyone feels that the referee was unfair, and verbal aggressions arise in the crowd. Just before they start fighting, the referee signals the end of the first half.

As they go to the dressing room, the coach yells in anger, "George!"

"George, what's the matter with you!?" screams Ruben, the team captain. "You had the opportunity and you missed it."

The coach tells him, "You can't continue playing if you don't concentrate. That was the third time this week."

George walks away, feeling down. He mutters to himself, "Problems, when will they end?" George continues walking towards the dressing room thinking about Lucy's party and his father's condition.

Ruben approaches George and asks him, "What made you lose your concentration during the game? Weren't you going to ask Miss Patty to help you deal with your problem?"

"Help me with my problem? Don't you know Miss Patty? I think she got me into more problems. I'd forgotten that she only gives hints. She says everybody should solve their own problems," George replies.

"Hints? What hints did she give you?" asks Ruben.

"It's a drawing with two figures. But, I can't relate that drawing with the problem I have with my parents," answers George.

"Look, I don't know. Pass me that green shirt over there, please," says Ruben in a rush, as he changes clothes.

George says, "Which green shirt? I don't see it."

"How don't you see it?" asks Ruben annoyed, "I can see it from here."

George insists, "I can't see anything."

Ruben says, "You can't see it from there but I can see it from here."

George steps up and walks to the corner, sees the shirt, and says, "Here it is. I found it." He throws it to Ruben. "The thing is that in many situations we can't see what another person sees unless we place ourselves in their position," murmurs George to himself. George starts to laugh.

"What's up with you? What are you laughing about? Weren't you just angry a few minutes ago?" asks Ruben.

"I figured out the answer to the drawing. It means that from my point of view I am sure of something. I defend my view because it is the only thing I can see. If each person sticks to what they see, and doesn't place themselves in the other person's shoes, we will never be able to solve our conflicts," answers George. "Oh... now I get it! I think the teacher was talking about the existence of **two points of view in conflict for the same situation.** It means that my parents stick to their point of view just like I do. But, who's right?"

"Look man, I don't know," replies Ruben.

"Hurry up! We are waiting for you." shouts Gabriel. "We have to go and win this game!"

Wednesday the 8th
9:45 AM

"Miss Patty!" yells George at Miss Patty as she walks quickly down the hall. She is a bit late because her history students asked her too many questions about her new way of teaching class. With her new methodology, she challenges her students to use their logic and become better critical thinkers. She believes this will help them study and improve their grades. She is using this new method because the performance of the class has begun to worry her.

"Miss Patty!" George insists once more.

Miss Patty turns around and is surprised that George is the one calling her. She assumed it was one of the pupils from her last class.

"George, what do you need?" she asks.

"I need to tell you that I understand what you where trying to tell me with the drawing. You meant that both parts can be right, but that does not solve my problem. I still want to go to the party, and my father still does not want to let me go. Considering his health status, we will never reach an agreement. **It is impossible for both *wants* to exist at the same time,**" George says.

"I would love to continue talking with you. I can see you are very enthusiastic, and I don't want to miss the whole story, but I am in a hurry. **Are our *wants* the only issue in our problems, or is there anything else?** Analyze that," says Miss Patty.

George thinks to himself, "Again with more questions... She really likes the intrigue." George stayed in the hallway thinking.

11:25 AM

In class, Lucy is very impatient waiting for a break. She has to find George, because she is not sure if he will be her date to her Sweet Sixteen party. Frankly, she does not know what to do. She feels a lot of pressure because she likes George a lot. Her mother insists on talking to George's parents, but Lucy does not want her parents to intervene, because she wants to be sure that George will not feel awkward.

Lucy is tall, thin, and very sweet. She has brown eyes and long hair. She is admired among her classmates because even though she is very pretty, she is humble and constantly happy. Lucy is the oldest of her family, and it will be the first big birthday party in her family. That is why the event has everyone so excited. Rachel, Lucy's mother, is very busy fixing every detail. She is not willing to lose control, because she wants to manage the party. Joseph, Lucy's father, has not been himself lately. Usually, he is a very reserved man. He is a hard worker with no sentimentalisms. He never thought an event like this would excite him so much.

11:30

Lucy is looking for George in the backyard. Although he is interested in her, he doesn't want to see her at this moment. Last weekend, Lucy invited him to be her date, but his father denied him permission. For George, it is inconceivable to tell her that he cannot go. That is why he is avoiding her.

George tries to hide, but she finds him anyways. "George, I need to talk to you," says Lucy.

George turns to face her, acting as if he didn't know she was there. "Hi Lucy. I didn't notice you were here," he says. He approaches Lucy slowly, thinking about what to say next.

"So, George, are you going to be able to be my date to the party?" she asks.

"I don't know yet. If you give me one more week, I promise you I'll have an answer. It is not that I don't want to go with you, but I have a family problem, and I hope I can resolve it with my parents."

"One week! That's impossible!" replies Lucy.

"What do you mean it is impossible? The party is in two weeks. Or is it that you don't want to wait for me?" asks George.

Lucy says, "It is not that I don't want to wait. Please understand… it is only two weeks from now. **I need to be sure, if not, I will have to invite another friend.** Imagine if I invited someone else at the last minute. I cannot do that! "

"What do you mean you **need** to be sure?" asks George.

"As I said, I do **want** you to be my date at my party. But if you don't tell me now, I will have to find someone else. I can't take that risk and wait until the day of the party to find another date! It would be so embarrassing!" says Lucy.

"So, it isn't that you don't **want** me to go?" asks George.

"Of course, I would love it if you could go with me. But, you have to understand that if you don't decide soon, I will have to go with another guy," replies Lucy.

"All right, I promise you this Friday I'll talk to my parents," says George.

"This time is for real. I'll wait, but only until Friday," says Lucy.

"Friday," said George to himself. "If she knew the problem I have with dad, she wouldn't be so demanding. But, now isn't the right time to tell her. She is worried enough with her party, and she really needs to know if she can count on me."

George stays there thinking. Somehow, he felt that this "**need**" stuff could be related to the "**wants**" he was thinking about earlier with Miss Patty.

So Miss Patty was talking about **needs**? Lucy was right. I have to answer her invitation at this moment so she knows someone will go with her to the party. That's her **need**. On the other hand, it's not right to respond to her invitation right now. Dad is sick, and I can't aggravate his situation even more. That is my **need**. That is what Miss Patty was talking about when she said that wants are not the only issue. In a conflict, people also have needs to be satisfied. **The thing is that in a conflict wants cannot coexist but needs could.** So, the problem is not on the **needs**, but on the **wants**. **Needs** are far more important than **wants**. That is what Miss Patty was talking about. I think I understand.

12:30 PM

George heads to the hospital. It's a short walk from school, and he could use the time to think about his situation. Now he has a clue regarding his and her **needs.**

George thinks to himself, "Although it is hard to admit, I'm thinking both of us are right. Now I just need to find my father's need. Why wouldn't he let me go? I have to place myself in his situation and think as he would. Maybe he doesn't want me to have fun. No. No. No, I don't think so. My father has always taken us places to have fun on vacations. That's not the answer. Why wouldn't he let me go? It's not easy understanding someone's **needs.**"

George starts to think about school. "Maybe they know I fall asleep in class. Although, I don't think that's the reason, because Miss Patty has never told me anything about it. I hope she has not noticed it. Maybe they found out about Irene's party when the Zafiro's gang fought our gang and Julian and Robert went straight to jail. The good thing is that nothing happened, but we were really scared…that must be it. I'm sure they already know. Parents communicate with other parents very often."

Then George gets a new idea. "Oh! I know! My grades! They have been unusually low lately. They must be scared and think I party too much!"

George arrives to the hospital and bumps into his mom at the elevator. She was lost in thought and didn't notice him.

"Hi mom," says George. "How's Dad doing? Have you talked to the doctors? Did they tell you what's wrong with him?"

Louise stares at him dropping a tear, "I am afraid things are not that simple."

"Why do you say that?" asks George.

"Because they keep running tests all the time," she replies.

"But, what do they tell you about the tests?" he asks.

"Nothing yet," says Louise.

George holds her and softly asks, "Where are you going?"

"I'm going to the cafeteria. Your brother is upstairs with your dad. I'm going to eat something. It's been a long morning and I need to get away for a while. Would you like to go with me?" she asks.

They head down to the cafeteria. They start to eat, and Louise notices George hasn't touched his food yet. "Why don't you eat? Did you eat something at school?" she asks.

"No. I'm not hungry," answers George thoughtfully.

Concerned about her son, Louise asks, "Is there anything wrong?"

"Yes. Do you remember that discussion with Dad?" he asks.

Louise replies, "Of course I remember but...."

George interrupts her, "Well, I haven't solved that issue, and I am very worried because I have to give Lucy an answer. I don't think it's the right moment for me to speak to Dad. I'm concerned about his health, but, on the other hand, Lucy can't wait for me any longer, because she needs to be sure she has a date for her birthday."

"Of course, she needs an answer right away," says Louise.

"Well, yes... How can I talk to Dad without affecting his health? Why do we always end up arguing? Why can't we get along?" he asks.

"Are you interested in getting along with your Dad?" asks Louise.

"Yeah... sure. It's obvious, but do you think Dad is interested in getting along with me?" asks George.

Louise starts to answer that question when Al arrives in a rush. "Mom!" says Al to Louise. "Results are back. The doctor is with Dad. Hurry up!"

George and Louise stand up and walk quickly to the elevator.

Meanwhile, Lucy and her friends are talking at Maggie's house about how to dress for the party. Maggie is Lucy's best friend. She is a caring person and is always worrying about the group. She is a brunette, average in height, and slightly overweight. She has brilliant brown, curly hair that falls behind her shoulders. She also has dark brown eyes and straight white teeth that make her smile very pleasant.

"Susie?" asks Maggie. "Do you know if your aunt can help us shop for the clothes for the party?"

"Yes, of course. But we need to decide now, since she is a very busy fashion designer."

"I want to wear purple!" yells Anna.

"No, that's the color of my top!" yells Lucy.

"Ok, then," says Susie to Lucy. "We should find a color that goes with your eyes. Maybe a salmon color would work."

"No. Salmon doesn't go with my hair," says Lucy worried.

Laura has been totally quiet. She seems to be sad, but nobody has noticed. After discussing for a while about the music for the party, Anna turns to Laura and asks, "What's wrong Laura? Are you alright?"

"Yes, I'm fine," she says with a short smile as she attempts to hide her sadness.

"Do you like the music we are choosing for the party?" Anna asks.

"No. It's not that," answers Laura. "I don't know how to tell you… I'm not going to be able to go to the party."

"What?" reacted the group.

"Why?" Lucy asked surprised.

Laura's eyes fill with tears. "It's obvious. How do you think I'm going to look? I am two sizes bigger than you!"

"Come on. Please, look at me," says Maggie. "We are almost the same, but I'm not worried about that, because I am happy the way I am."

"It is going to be so embarrassing," answers Laura.

"I'll give you my diet. I guarantee you will lose weight in one month," says Susie.

"But, who will want to take me? I went through this in middle school, and I ended up taking my cousin, because three guys rejected my invitation. I'm not willing to do that again," says Laura.

"Oh, Laura, I wish that was my problem," says Anna. "Don't worry. Imagine if I would have given up a long time ago. I probably wouldn't be here enjoying these moments," says Anna. The girls sat there in silence with their eyes filled up with tears.

Anna was born with an incurable disease called Lymphoma. She had surgery when she was two-months-old and had a large part of her intestine removed. She has surgery every so often, to remove tumors from her body. These procedures are very painful, and she has to follow a strict diet. More than once, she has had to struggle for her life. Although her treatment has been painful, she has set an example for everyone in her life. Her enthusiasm, joy, generosity, and desire to live have let her focus on the positive things in her life. She has discovered the essential value of the ones around her, and that's why she can love unconditionally.

"There are far more important things in life. Real beauty is not about looks or clothes. It's about who you really are. You're a really nice person, and you're very valuable to your parents and friends. The key to happiness is to accept yourself the way you are. This will help you to accept everyone else. You need to be thankful and learn to enjoy every moment. Remember, nobody knows their time in life. Seize the day," says Anna.

Everyone sheds a tear of joy as they hug each other. Anna's words stayed deep in their hearts, filling them with joy and a new attitude towards life.

11:00 PM

George tries to sleep, but the problems he is dealing with won't let him. His father's condition and Lucy's party make him feel uneasy. Al says there's nothing to worry about, and George starts to see the light. He has learned that in a problem **both parties have valid needs.** When one person defends what he or she **wants,** it is only because he or she has a **need** to be satisfied. He understands that he needs to place himself in the other person's position to comprehend it, but he doesn't understand how to resolve the problem. Is there anything else to learn?

"I remember something a teacher once told me: 'Chaos is the beginning of order.' I think I'm beginning to understand," George says to himself.

Thursday the 9th
1:00 PM

"Ruben, wait!" yells Gabriel as he arrives at school. "Have you thought about what we are going to do about this weekend?"

Gabriel is good-looking, average in height, and a formal dresser. He is impulsive and enthusiastic. Since he finished middle school, he has been working at his father's business. Gabriel's father thinks young boys should start working so they can develop a sense of responsibility. Gabriel's grades don't reflect his true intelligence.

"Don't say it out loud. The jocks at that table are going to hear you. I haven't thought of how we are going to get out of this problem yet. Things are turning ugly on us. We should get together and discuss it," says Ruben.

"What should we do?" asks Gabriel.

"I don't know. We should get together to agree on something," says Ruben.

"We'll organize a meeting after school at the hamburger place," says Gabriel.

"There goes Maggie and Susie. Let's go talk to them," says Ruben.

"Maggie! Susie! Wait for me!" yells Gabriel trying to reach them. "We are going to have lunch at the hamburger place after school. Spread the word. We need to talk about the Zafiros incident. It's urgent!"

Maggie and Susie head quickly to the bathroom, saying that they need to freshen up before their math class. They thought they were alone, but they were so nervous they didn't notice Miss Patty was also in the bathroom.

"Do you realize this thing is serious? We are in deep trouble," says Maggie to Susie.

"What are we going to do? What if they bring weapons?" asks Susie.

"Remember what Mr. Luis said. These guys are dangerous. They have confronted the police. Hurry up! Let's go tell everybody about lunch at the hamburger place," says Maggie.

They rush out of the bathroom. Miss Patty is intrigued from what she heard and is worried about the safety of her students. She thinks about how she can help them.

1:15 PM

George enters his math class and heads toward the end of the room. He hopes to find a place to sit and rest for a while without being seen by the teacher. "My head is a mess," thinks George. "And the last thing I can tolerate at this moment is equations. I could miss class, but I have too many absences and I don't want to get in trouble."

He stares at the teacher to pretend he is paying attention, but he isn't. "I'm running out of time," continues George in his thoughts. "I should start solving my problems now. Otherwise, they're going to grow bigger. First, I need to talk to Dad. The easiest thing would be telling Lucy I'm not going to her party. No way! That's impossible! I'm talking to Dad today. That's decided. But, how can I bring up the subject without him going nuts? Is he healthy enough to handle this? If I start talking about the party, I'm afraid he is going to faint again. I have to start with something that doesn't make him mad. For example..."

"George! Pay attention! After the exam you are going to say you didn't see this material in class," the teacher says. "Let's find the common denominator," he says to the class.

George goes back to thinking, repeating the words he just heard: "A common denominator...**Common?**" George thinks and suddenly the bell rings. All his classmates are dismissed. George remains seated as he continues to think. The word common revolves around his head. He wonders why that word reminds him of the conversation he had with his mom regarding the situation with his father.

"Oh, I know. Even if dad and I have a conflict, we still have a **common objective** as a family! I should find a way to speak to dad with something that we both agree on— something that makes us want to solve the conflict. Brilliant! Who would've said that math could help me in real life?" George laughs to himself

2:05 PM

Miss Patty rushes to the hamburger restaurant. When she sees the big group of boys, she starts to worry even more. She thought the problem involved only three or four.

"What are you celebrating? Why didn't you invite me?" asks Miss Patty, pretending she doesn't know anything.

Everyone freezes. It is a real surprise to see Miss Patty. They start to ask themselves, "Does she know anything? Maybe somebody told her or perhaps it's just a coincidence." Nobody dares to answer her question.

Miss Patty notices their nervousness and asks, "What's the matter? I see you are worried. Maybe you are organizing something I shouldn't know about. I don't want to interrupt. I'd better go. If you need my help you know you can count on me."

Miss Patty heads to the counter to order a hamburger. "No. Wait!" says Maggie. "I think Miss Patty can help us."

"What is it?" asks Miss Patty as she sits down.

"You see Miss Patty, last weekend we went to Gabriel's ranch to celebrate his birthday," starts Andrew nervously. "After lunch we ran out of chips as usual."

"Hold on a second," Miss Patty interrupts. "I need to order my hamburger. If I don't eat now, I'll get cranky." After ordering her hamburger, she asks them to continue.

"Well as I said, we went to the convenience store right off the highway. Peter, Gabriel's oldest brother, went to buy the chips while we talked about the soccer game we'd watched on TV. Suddenly, the Zafiros came out of the store and started joking with us. You know the Zafiros. They're that group of trouble makers that are always picking fights and are known to be involved in criminal acts. Anyways,

John made a bad comment about their favorite team and that made them angry. They started yelling at us. Luis Oviedo, the owner of the store, heard the noise and came out to warn us. We jumped into our cars and one of them approached Gabriel and threatened him. Gabriel says he has no clue why they are angry with him. The Zafiros got near our car and one of them yelled: 'We'll see you on Saturday outside the Hawk Bar at eight o'clock. We'll see if you can defend yourselves without Mr. Oviedo.' Mr. Oviedo stepped out of the convenience store with Peter and warned us about those boys. He said they were trouble makers and that the police had already scared them. He said we should be very careful around them."

"Miss Patty, we don't know what to do! We are very worried about this, and we can't concentrate on the exams. We have math on Monday, and we can't afford to fail the test" says Susie.

"We have to go," says Gabriel. "Imagine what they would say if we didn't show up. I won't let them say I am scared. What's wrong with showing up? If we go, we'll show them we're not afraid," he insists.

"Besides, they can't handle us. We are way too strong," added Andrew.

"Andrew, this isn't the moment to act manly. You have to put your feet on the ground and look at the possible unintended consequences. I already have enough trouble with my parents without being a part of this," says George.

"Unintended consequences...? Come on George! What consequences can this bring to us?" says Andrew.

"What consequences did you have for not taking the uniform to the soccer game?" asks Miss Patty to Andrew.

"Don't remind me about that. I'm still angry. Coach didn't let me play," answers Andrew.

"**Do you realize that any action can generate a chain of events**? Sometimes these consequences lead us to positive or negative results," says Miss Patty.

"In this case, I don't see any negative consequences," responds Andrew.

"Are you blind or what? What if they beat us up?" says Maggie.

"No," says Hurley. "The worst thing that could happen is getting kicked out of school."

"That's the worst?" asks Miss Patty.

"Kicked out of school!" says Luis nervously.

"You are overreacting," says John. "That's not going to happen. I think you are going too far. Don't exaggerate."

"You seem very sure John. Are you psychic or what?" asks Ernie.

"Wait a minute. I know you are very nervous, but everybody talking at the same time doesn't get us anywhere," says Miss Patty as she tries to calm down the group.

"Don't you think if we go to the bar they're going to look for a fight?" insisted Luis.

"But why?" asks Miss Patty.

"When a guy challenges someone, it's to see which one is stronger," replied Hurley.

"Of course, that's very important. Every **cause** has an **effect**, because there's an **assumption, reason or explanation**," says Miss Patty to Hurley.

Everyone starts talking at the same time. "Wait a minute. Let's organize these ideas," says Miss Patty. "If you show up, they'll think you want to fight, as Luis says. That sounds logical."

"Yes, it sounds logical," says Luis. "But if we go, they're going to provoke us," says John.

"Sure. We said that every action creates a series of events, or reactions. Do you remember, John?" says Miss Patty. "But why, John? Give a reason."

"Because that's what they're looking for," answers John.

"And if they provoke you, what's going to happen?" asks Miss Patty.

"We'll start to fight," says Andrew.

"Can anybody give me a reason?" asks Miss Patty.

"Sure. The reason is we have to defend ourselves," answers Luis.

"And then?" asks Miss Patty.

"They'll beat us up, because they don't fight fairly," yelled Gabriel.

"Have you noticed that you're giving me the reasons?" says Miss Patty.

"If they beat us up, things can get really nasty. They might pull out weapons," says George.

"So?" Andrew challenges.

"Isn't that enough? We can end up in the hospital or dead," says Ernie.

"We can end up in jail and with a criminal record!" says George.

"Sure. And everyone at school will find out," says Maggie.

"It's obvious they will expel us from school," says Luis in a worried tone.

"If the Zafiros don't kill me, my parents will!" says Ernie.

"I don't want to be punished or expelled," says Luis.

"Of course not!" everyone yells.

"I never thought this could happen. **I'm not used to thinking about future consequences**," says Ernie.

"What if we show up and refuse to fight?" asks Maggie.

"Impossible!" John says.

"Why? We have to find a way to let them know we are not willing to fight," says Maggie.

"What will happen if you show up and refuse to fight?" asks Miss Patty.

"All the negative things that we have said might not happen," answers Maggie.

"How can you show up and not get into a fight?" asks Miss Patty.

"I don't know Miss Patty. What do you have in mind?" asks Maggie.

"I've got a couple of ideas Maggie. However, when somebody has a problem, he is the only one that can fix it. I can only be the mediator. So, my advice is to think about it all afternoon. I trust you. I'm sure you'll make the right decision," says Miss Patty.

"Miss Patty, this is like what we were doing in history class," says Anna.

"What do you mean Anna?" asks Miss Patty.

"Like that example we saw about Native American History," says Anna.

Miss Patty smiles and asks Anna, "Do you remember?"

"Sure I do. If the Europeans attacked the Indians, logically they defended themselves," says Anna.

"Do you remember the reason?" asks Miss Patty.

"Yes. The Indians had to defend their land," says Anna.

"As you can see, analyzing consequences is a practice you can use in class and in everyday situations to help find the best alternative solution. You now know the tool and can make the analysis. It is up to you whether this situation ends up badly or not. Remember: **COURAGE is not demonstrated through AGGRESSION, but through reason**," say Miss Patty.

"You're right, Miss Patty. I think it's our best option. It's important that we analyze this situation. I don't want to be expelled from school," says Luis.

4:00 PM

George is in his room. His mother, father, and brother are in the hospital. He hasn't been alone in his house for a long time. Since he started high school, he has come home only to sleep. His friends, homework, and soccer have kept him very busy.

George thinks to himself, "I have to get the things mom needs at the hospital. If I don't concentrate, I'm going to forget something. I didn't bring up the party issue last time, and we actually didn't argue. I can finally talk to dad without fighting. I can't ruin things now. I need him to be happy so that I can get his permission."

George heads to the hospital, optimistic and hopeful that he will be able to talk to his dad now that things aren't so bad. The doctor's analysis, even though it was only a preliminary exam, gave everyone a lot of hope. On the other hand, his dad already forgave him, so everything is peaceful now.

George keeps practicing what he'll say to his dad during the walk to the hospital when he realizes he's already there. When he gets into the room, he sees his uncles, his father's brothers. Although he is very glad to see them, he feels disappointed, because he won't have a chance to speak to his dad alone. When they finally say goodbye, he feels relieved, shuts the door, and stays alone with his dad. George is a little bit nervous and thinks, "It is now or never."

"Dad," George says. "You look very good. How was your day?"

"Better, I just hope that future analyses are as good as the preliminary ones. Right now I feel like new. You'll still have a dad for a long time…I hope," says Frank.

"Me too," George says. "I hope now we can understand each other better. What do you think?"

"I want to get along with you. I'm sorry I hurt you. It's just that your mom and I sometimes forget that we were also teenagers once," says Frank.

"I understand you get worried because my grades have never been this bad. I know that's the reason you won't let me go to Lucy's party," George says.

"Now you're getting it!" his dad says, astonished that George actually understands. "This month has been the worst. Your grades have never been so low. Of course, you also have been at too many parties and activities. And you are involved in everything! Have you seen yourself in a mirror? You look like you're not sleeping well," says Frank.

George sits on his dad's bed. "I don't have anything against you going to parties," his dad continues, while putting his arm around him. "And I think it is good to be involved in sports and go out with your friends. But, we are really worried."

"You have a right to worry," George cheerfully says as he sees his dad opening up. "But dad, this party is special...."

"Why is it so important to you?" his dad interrupts.

"Dad, what would you do if you were me? Lucy is the most popular girl at school, and she chose me to be her date. I can't say no! If I say no, she will think I'm not interested, and that's not true, because I'm very interested."

"So that means you are thinking about having a girlfriend?" asks Frank.

The door opens. It is the nurse bringing dinner.

Friday the 10th
7:50AM

George is walking to class with a big smile. He bumps into Hurley who asks, "Hey George? Why are you so happy? If we've got that appointment with the Zafiros, do you know what we're going to do?"

"I fixed my issues with my dad!" George answers enthusiastically.

"Didn't you hear me? I'm talking about the problem with the Zafiros," Hurley repeats.

"Problem with the Zafiros? The ones with my dad are real problems, and I never thought that we'd be able to solve them. He's so stubborn. And now we are friends," replies George.

"How did you do it?" asks Hurley.

"We reached an agreement and now I understand what Miss Patty told me. There are **win-win** solutions!" George says. "What I learned when talking to my Dad was about **assumptions**…Sometimes we assume things that aren't correct. Once you figure those out, your conflicts tend to disappear."

"You are talking deep stuff now. Are you high?" Hurley says smiling, "have you being reading mystic stuff? I don't understand a bit of what you're talking about," Hurley continues.

"Let me explain," replied George. "Remember my little cousin, Jessica?"

"Yes, the one that looks like you," recalls Hurly.

"Yes that's the one," George agrees. "People used to tell her that, but then she would cry."

"That's because you are ugly," Hurley says jokingly.

"Shut up and let me finish" yells George. "I asked her one day why she cried, and do you know what she said? She said because they were saying that she looked like a boy. You see, she has a wrong assumption," George emphasizes.

"So, did you solve the problem?" Hurley asked.

"Yes, I told her that what they really meant was that I look like a girl," George says. "After that her attitude changed...anytime someone would tell her that she looks like me, she would smile," George says.

"Yeah you are onto something," Hurley agrees.

"**One should continuously challenge one's assumptions**," George concludes.

"Ok," says Hurley. "Now tell me, if you were able to fix your problem with your dad, do you think you can now fix the one with the Zafiros? Let's see if you can now concentrate on this problem. Remember, we need to dedicate some time to Miss Patty's analysis. It's imperative that we solve this."

"We can get together later. Right now, I need to run to class to do history homework, and today is the last day. Did you do it?" asks George.

"No. I didn't finish it, because I was too busy trying to solve all the problems. We still have time. The teachers are in a meeting. Remember, it's Friday and all the teachers get together to gossip about what we did during the week," says Hurley.

They keep thinking about how to solve the problem with the Zafiros.

8:15 AM

Miss Patty comes out of the teachers' meeting very discontented. "It's always the same!" she thinks to herself as she walks to her history class. "Every semester is the same thing! The same problem that we all know: **OUR STUDENTS' GRADES ARE DROPPING DOWN!** We understand that the transition from junior high to high school is always hard for the boys, especially during the first semester. It always happens that their grades drop down considerably or do not improve as expected."

Parents always think that it's because high school has a different system than junior high. But that's not the only reason. There are many other factors that add up. It seems that parents forget the age of their kids. These kids want to be independent, and they start experiencing the taste of freedom. Parents don't remember when they were that age.

Teenagers have many distractions that are more important to them than studying. That's why it's difficult for parents to understand why they don't study. On the other hand, teenagers don't understand that finishing high school is a requirement if they want to go to college.

Miss Patty has been thinking about this problem since last semester. But this semester, she wants to prevent it from happening again. Miss Patty has told her students many times: "We should not settle with mediocrity. To succeed in life, we need to break boundaries." Now is time to prove that this is right. She has decided to make her students improve their grades. To accomplish this task, Miss Patty made a proposal at the teachers' meeting and it was accepted. Nevertheless, it was not enough because students also need to make a commitment to make this change. We want to solve their problems, but it won't be successful if they don't cooperate and make the necessary changes.

When she arrives in the classroom, she sees the students rushing to finish their papers that are due today. "Procrastinators," she thinks. "They leave everything for the last minute."

"Good morning," says Miss Patty.

"Good morning," a few of the students barely answer.

"Good morning!" she repeats enthusiastically. Miss Patty is trying to get all the students to answer.

"Good morning," answers the class as they finish their papers.

"Stop your work," says Miss Patty. "I have news for you from the teachers' meeting."

"What are you up to now? A new punishment?" asks John.

"A trip to Orlando sounds like a punishment to you?" Miss Patty replies.

When they hear the word "trip" everyone sits up properly to hear what Miss Patty has to say next. "Where? When?" everyone asks.

"Who will go on that trip?" asks Susie.

"The class with the best average," says Miss Patty.

"So, we're not going!" yells Hurley.

Everyone gets anxious and disappointed.

"No way, Miss Patty. That's impossible!" says Maggie.

"Why do you say that?" Miss Patty asks Maggie.

"Oh Miss Patty, come on. The genius students are in class number five," interrupts George.

"Genius students?" asks Miss Patty "That means that you are…?"

Nobody answers.

"I've been analyzing each one of your capacities," continues Miss Patty. "And I noticed that you are not using them."

"Oh, Miss Patty, we don't have the best teachers. Well, except for you, of course," says Lucy. "But, I still think it's impossible."

"Impossible? Why?" asks Miss Patty.

Everyone starts talking at the same time, trying to give their points of view to the teacher. "Wait a moment!" says Miss Patty loudly, as she tries to get everybody's attention. "If you talk all at the same time, I won't be able to understand what you are saying."

Gabriel raises his hand and asks, "What will happen if some of us are not interested in going on the trip?"

"We won't be able to make it. Only the class with best average is going," says Luis to his classmates.

"We have to work as a team," says Ruben.

"You finally said something smart!" jokes John.

"Raise your hand if you agree to try," continues Ruben, very interested in this new opportunity.

Suddenly, everyone starts raising their hand, except for Hurley. "What's wrong Hurley? Why don't you raise your hand?" asks Maggie, unimpressed by her friend's attitude.

"I don't get it. What is it that we are going to do as a team?" asks Hurley as he looks at his classmates.

"Improve our grades," responds Luis.

"No," says Lucy. "That's not enough. We have to get the best average."

"Of course, that's the condition to take the trip," says Maggie.

"You're right Maggie. *The best average* is our **last prerequisite** to accomplish our goal, which is going on that trip," Miss Patty tells her students. "So that means that…" she says as she walks towards the board, "our **ambitious target** is…."

"Getting the best group average," answers everyone at the same time.

"The best group average from all high school?" asks Luis.

"No, only from your grade level," responds Miss Patty as she writes *GETTING THE BEST GROUP AVERAGE FROM THE SAME GRADE LEVEL* on the blackboard. "It is important that we all agree this is our goal" insists Miss Patty. "Are we all in this together?" she continues.

"Yeah!" answers the whole class.

"Getting the best group average," says Susie with disbelief. "Sounds easy but...."

"Oh Miss Patty, that's not going to be easy" says John.

Miss Patty's students think that the **goal or ambitious target** is too big for them to accomplish. Until now, nobody had proposed anything like this to them. They are not used to giving their opinion about something. And they're not sure if they are going to be taken seriously. The students begin to wonder, "Is something wrong with Miss Patty? Is she up to something? What's she going to ask us to do?"

"Miss Patty, what do we win by giving our points of view? Since when are we taken seriously?" some students ask.

Suddenly, Andrew stands up and says, "It's not that we don't want to Miss Patty. It's that we can't."

"You can't, or you don't want to?" Miss Patty replies.

"Of course we want to!" says Luis.

"Who's not going to want to improve their average? That will end the discussions with our parents!" says George.

"So? **Who or what is stopping you now?**" Miss Patty challenges the class.

Everyone starts talking at the same time again. Hurley stands up and says, "Miss Patty, there are a lot of things that stop us from accomplishing our goal."

"I can see that you all want to talk. But, we are going to do it one by one. Each one of you will get the opportunity to tell me why we can't accomplish our goal. Remember, though, we are going to work as a team. Each one of you has your own **obstacles.** Now it is your time to complain all you want about those obstacles," explains Miss Patty.

"Finally, someone who understands us!" says Hurley. "I like that."

"Ok, let's start," says Miss Patty. She writes the word OBSTACLES on the board. "Who would like to write all the obstacles on the board?" she asks her students. Lucy stands up quickly and heads to the board.

"Hurley, tell us your obstacle!" says Miss Patty.

"I don't like some of the subjects we study," answers Hurley.

"But, you are always absent. How do you know?" asks Susie.

"Wait a minute, I told you that each one of you is going to be able to talk, but no one has the right to speak for the other," says Miss Patty.

"Don't say that Susie. I always ask someone for the notes," says Hurley.

"And I guess that's enough. Isn't it?" asks Miss Patty.

"No, it isn't," George responds, ashamed of his own actions.

"Continue Ruben," says Miss Patty.

"We don't understand some of the teachers," says Ruben.

"They give us a lot of homework and we don't finish on time," says Luis.

"Some of the teachers are not good at explaining," says George.

"They don't explain or you are asleep?" interrupts Susie.

George gives a bad look to Susie and explains, "I don't have the complete notes."

"Luis, continue," says Miss Patty.

"I don't see any other obstacle Miss Patty," he says.

"Think about it. Remember, this is team work. We have to think. If we don't find an obstacle, later on something will show up and we won't be able to accomplish our goal. Take your time, and I will ask you again later," Miss Patty explains.

The list of obstacles starts to grow. Nevertheless, Miss Patty needs to be sure everyone expresses their obstacles.

"Your turn, Maggie," says Miss Patty.

"I can't study at home with my brother's music playing so loud. He has a karaoke machine. He thinks he could be on American Idol," Maggie answers as everyone laughs.

"The library is closed during the afternoon, and it is the only time I can come to study," says Lucy as she writes her obstacle on the board.

"What about my obstacle, Miss Patty?" says Gabriel. "I have to help my father at the store."

"Thank you, Gabriel," says Miss Patty. "Have you thought about it, Luis?"

"Yes, Miss Patty. Not everyone works as hard as I do. When we work in teams, I always work harder than the rest, and I end up doing everything by myself."

"Alright! Anyone else?" continues Miss Patty.

"You don't think that's enough?" asks Lucy. "I don't have enough space to write more."

Miss Patty then says, "You can write them on the other board. We have to make sure we don't forget something! Let's start over again! Everyone must give a second obstacle."

When they finish giving their second obstacles, Andrew asks, "Now what? What are we going to do with so many obstacles?"

"What will happen if you have a game and the defender doesn't show up? Could you play anyway?" Miss Patty asks.

"Of course," says Ruben.

"And how would you do it?" continues Miss Patty.

"The substitute will play," says Gabriel.

"And if he doesn't show up?" insists Miss Patty.

"We will look for someone who could take that place," interrupts Ruben.

"And that way you can play?" asks Miss Patty again.

"Sure!" says Ernie.

"So, what did you do with the obstacle?" asks Miss Patty.

"We looked for the way to overcome it," says Maggie.

"Exactly! All of those obstacles are like little rocks in our way. It is up to us, if we stumble on them, to remove them or walk around them in our quest to reach our ambitious target," explains Miss Patty.

"It's like when we won the soccer championship. We first had to eliminate the other teams before we could go to the championship," says George.

"But, you didn't play against all the teams in the league at the same time," says Susie. "You had to play against one at a time. Let me see if I got it, Miss Patty. **This means that to accomplish a goal we have to achieve a bunch of smaller goals**. Right?"

"Right Susie," smiles Miss Patty. "So, let's turn every obstacle into **intermediate objectives**. For example, Ernie, if the obstacle is that you don't like certain subjects, the intermediate objective will be...?"

"Well..." thinks Ernie.

Everyone starts answering, but Miss Patty interrupts, "When someone has an obstacle, he or she has to find the solution."

"Make studying fun?" Ernie answers indecisively.

"Very good!" affirms Miss Patty. "Ok, now each one of you will write on the board next to your obstacles the intermediate objective," continues Miss Patty.

"This is strange. Each one of these intermediate objectives doesn't look so difficult," says Hurley.

"Yes," replied Miss Patty. "**Breaking down a goal into smaller parts is a first step to accomplishing great things**. Just think about how ants build their colonies...one little rock at a time."

"Yeah right, Miss Patty. Everything sounds okay now, but what's next?" asks Luis.

"And, who do you think this depends on? Who will stop you from accomplishing them?" questions Miss Patty.

Everyone quiets down. They understand that it's up to them to achieve their goals, and that no one is going to do it for them.

"What are we going to do with these intermediate objectives?" says Luis.

"If we already have all of the intermediate objectives," says Maggie. "Where should we start?"

"In order to get to high school, what did you have to do first?" asks Miss Patty.

"Finish junior high," says Susie.

"But first elementary," says Maggie.

"In that case, **logically**, preschool was first," says Ruben.

"Precisely," says Miss Patty. "So, what do we have to do with our **intermediate objectives**?"

"Put them in logical sequence," says George.

"Right!" says Miss Patty, satisfied. "Now, for homework each one of you will accommodate the objectives in logical sequence, and that way we will be able to know what the plan will be. We are going to make a map. Every step on the map is necessary to accomplish the next. That way, we will attack one intermediate objective at a time and finally accomplish our **AMBITIOUS TARGET**."

The bell rings while the students continue working. Miss Patty has never seen them so enthusiastic during class. This is the first time that they suggested the steps to be followed. Now that they are the protagonist, they accepted the challenge. This is real team work. Each one of them is responsible for accomplishing their own intermediate objectives.

11:45 AM

They all go out to lunch and, little by little, they gather at the same place. They are still nervous because they need to decide what they are going to do with their Zafiros appointment. It's tomorrow.

"Well, now we are all here," says Raul.

"No, not everyone is here. Lucy is missing," confirms Maggie.

"And so is George," says Andrew.

"I'll get them," Gabriel says in an agitated tone.

"Don't Go! They're talking about Lucy's party," says Andrew.

"Now what? Will he go with her? What happened with his dad? Did he recover? Was George able to get permission?" Susie asks with curiosity.

"But what's going to happen tomorrow?" Gabriel interrupts nervously.

Suddenly, George and Lucy arrive.

"George, what did you decide about tomorrow?" insists Gabriel.

"Don't count on me," George firmly says. "I don't want any more trouble."

"Me either," Ernie quickly answers.

"I insist that we go!" Andrew shouts.

"I was talking with my dad about what Miss Patty told us," says Gabriel. "He said, '**Whoever uses his brains instead of his fists is a better person**.' If we go, this will never end. They are trouble makers, and they'll look for any excuse to fight with us again. We need to end this now, without fighting!"

"Besides, we already have a very clear ambitious target that we all committed to. This is team work, and if one gets hurt, there's no way we can achieve the goal and win the prize," says Luis.

"Don't be sissies, "Andrew insists. "You don't want to be my friends any more?"

George gets angry, loses control, and stands in front of Andrew, "Then what? Do you want to spend the night in jail? Have a criminal record? End up at a hospital? Or at least get expelled and throw away everything we have accomplished so far? Are you willing to suffer the consequences? Fighting is not the only way to prove our friendship!"

Andrew says nothing.

"Well, then what do we do?" asks Lucy.

Everyone starts giving possible solutions and they finally decide what to do.

Saturday the 11th
12:30PM

George barely catches his breath. He is so worried about his problems, and if things weren't bad enough, he arrives home and gets the bad news that his dad is back in intensive care. He drops his things and runs out of the house. He grabs the first taxi that he sees and rushes to the hospital. The hospital is just a few blocks from home, but he doesn't want to lose one more second. "This can't happen. It can't happen again to my dad," George thinks with a tear in his eye. "Now that we finally get along!" He quietly starts praying.

He arrives and everyone is in his father's room. Well, everyone except his dad.

"What happened? What happened to dad?" George yells out of control.

"He had a crisis," Louise barely responds. "He went to the operation room."

"He went under the knife? But he was doing so well a few hours ago," George says.

"Yes, but calm down, he is recovering and he is far from any danger," continues Louise. Louise starts explaining what the doctors said after the last tests. Frank has had a clogged artery for many years and they needed to fix it with surgery. The doctor explained that this was due to the lack of physical activity, a careless diet, and the fact that he started smoking at a very young age. George can't avoid recalling what Miss Patty said: "Actions can generate a chain of events." How true this is now for my dad. George reflects.

George was finally able to catch his breath. He felt guilty about all that was happening to his dad. But, he finally understood that it wasn't his fault. George thinks about how to help his dad recover even faster.

4:00 PM

Maggie called Sergio and his brother Dan, both members of the Zafiros, and told them to meet her at the hamburger place at 5:00 p.m.

"Maggie, are you sure that your friends are coming?" George anxiously asks.

"Yes," Maggie responds. "I trust them."

"Look, there's Sergio," Marcela says while pointing towards him, "and also Dan."

"I hope this doesn't make things worse," says George quietly.

Sergio approaches Marcela. "Hey, what's up?" Sergio says.

"I'm glad you came, we need to talk," Marcela responds.

"Are you ready for tonight?" asks Sergio.

"We want to talk about that," George responds.

"You are stepping out? Are you afraid?" Sergio insists.

"No. We are neither afraid, nor do we regret anything. We have been thinking over this situation, and there's no way we want to fight. We won't jeopardize everything we've accomplished just because of a stupid fight," says George.

"What do you mean by 'jeopardizing everything you've accomplished'?" asks Sergio.

"Have you realized what could happen if we fight?" George insists.

"Are you afraid of losing?" Dan says

"No, it's not FEAR, it's just that we'll all end up losing," says George.

"Losing? Us...losing? We are stronger than you," Dan responds aggressively.

"What if the police arrive and arrest us? Isn't that losing something?" George asks.

"What if someone ends up at the hospital?" asks Lucy

"We could get expelled from high school," Gabriel says.

"Sergio, didn't you tell me that your dream was to be a lawyer?" Marcela asks, as she looks straight into Sergio's eyes. "You don't think you are risking something?"

Sergio and Dan quietly think about all that has been said.

"The truth is that you are sissies!" Dan continues.

"Think whatever you want, but we prefer to be called sissies instead of losing everything we've accomplished," George loudly responds.

"Didn't your uncle die recently in a fight, Dan?" Gabriel asks. Gabriel didn't want to mention this, but he had no other option.

"Don't you realize all the suffering that this has brought to your family? To your aunt? Cousins? Do you want to end up like him?" Marcela asks.

Dan starts feeling sad about all the memories revolving around that incident. He can't remove the image of his aunt when she found out about it. And, he'll always remember his cousin's face on the day they buried his uncle.

"So, you don't accept the challenge?" asks Sergio.

"NO!" all three firmly respond.

7:00 PM

Miss Patty is at her house, and she's very nervous. She is wondering what decision her students made. She is thinking about calling the police, or maybe some of the students' parents. She tells the whole story to her husband, who is also a teacher. But, she knows that her kids are capable of solving this without any confrontation. She has worked with them so much that she feels involved. All she can do is wait until Monday and trust whatever her students decided.

A FEW DAYS BEFORE THE PARTY

Time feels like it has passed very quickly. The students have been very busy studying for the exams, preparing for the party, striving toward their ambitious target, working on improving their grades, and going to soccer practice. They were so busy that they didn't realize that the party was this weekend.

After Lucy's Party

10:30 AM

They all get together like always for lunch at the same place under the shade of a big, old tree. They are very excited, and they all have something to say about the party. They have been talking about it all day.

"Lucy," says Marcela. "Your party was the best ever. You were right to have your mom decorate. She did an amazing job. Everything was perfect. I couldn't stop dancing the whole night!"

"The music was the best part," Hurley adds. "Having a live band was the best idea!"

George interrupts Hurley while staring at Lucy's eyes, "No Hurley, you are wrong. The best part was Lucy. She looked marvelous."

"Of course she did!" Susie and Laura say at the same time.

"Thanks guys. But if you weren't there, the party wouldn't have been that great," Lucy says as her face turns pink from blushing.

"My parents were also very happy for you Lucy," George says.

"How's your dad doing?" asks Lucy.

"He's much better. He just needs to rest, quit smoking, and follow a strict diet. I told him all about the party, and he was really happy. He can't wait to see the pictures," George says.

"By the way, when will you print the pictures?" asks Susie. "I can't wait to see them."

"I'll have them next week. We should get together to see them," says Lucy.

"We can get together at my place," says Maggie.

"Good idea! I like your place. Your mom always has snacks and drinks for us," Laura says enthusiastically.

"Now, I'm hungry," says Luis.

"Hey Laura, you looked great in that outfit. The color made you look very pretty," Anna comments.

"I know. Susie's aunt found the pants to match my top. And my date was awesome. My feet hurt from so much dancing," Laura says smiling. "I want to thank you Anna.

What you told me the other day made all the difference. I never really believed that the value of each one of us is inside and not on the outside. If I had only realized that a few years ago...."

"Hey Lucy, congratulations... it's about time George had a girlfriend. He was starting to drive us crazy," Ruben says to make fun of George.

Suddenly, Miss Patty walks by and sees everyone sitting under the tree. She asks, "And now what, are you still talking about the party or is there something new?"

"Well... Lucy and George are FINALLY a couple!!" responds Susie very happily.

"Oh, how romantic," sighs Miss Patty. "I wish I were a young girl again."

THREE MONTHS LATER on the last day of school

Miss Patty enters the classroom. Her students are intrigued because they want to know which classroom got the highest average. As soon as Miss Patty sat in her chair, the students ask her, "Who won the trip Miss Patty?"

"I don't know yet," she answers.

"You already know, but you don't want to tell us," says Maggie.

"What did you think about the final exams?" asks Miss Patty.

"They were easier than ever. I think that the teachers are getting better. They are finally taking our position," says John.

"The exams were easier? That's weird!" says Miss Patty.

"The exams haven't changed," says Luis.

"The thing is that I understand everything now," says George.

"Of course you do. You don't sleep anymore during class!" yells Susie, smiling.

"Well, it's because I sleep better at home now," answers George.

"Luis helped me," says John. "We got together after classes and studied in teams."

"I learned how to take notes," express George proudly.

"Are these the only things that you have accomplished during this semester?" asks Miss Patty.

"No," says Laura. "I felt lonely before, and now I know I can count on the group."

"It's more fun when we study together," says John.

"The good thing is that when we work as a team, everyone is responsible for their own tasks," says Luis.

"I convinced myself that I can get good grades," says Ernie.

"Before this, nobody listened to me. Now, they know my ideas are important too," expresses Andrew.

"We've learned to organize our time better," continues Maggie.

"The thing is that we all committed to getting this done," says George.

"We all cared about achieving this goal," continues Luis.

"I think that everything you said about the process to achieve an **AMBITIOUS TARGET** works," says Anna.

"Besides Hurley, did anyone else improve his or her grades?" asks Miss Patty.

"Of course," says Ruben. "My parents even congratulated me."

"Are you aware of how many skills and values you have developed without even noticing?" asks Miss Patty. "You learned that when we commit to accomplishing a goal, just fighting for it enriches us. That's because even though we may not be able to accomplish the goal, we experienced a great amount of valuable moments that make us grow as people."

"Yes, Miss Patty. We probably didn't have the time to accomplish this target, but I think that if we set our target on the first day of next semester, we can accomplish it," says Ruben.

"Miss Patty, we don't want to go. It is amazing how we've been able to learn in such a different way. There were tears, laughter, victories, and failures. Just like in an adventure. I think we could write a book about it," Hurley emotionally comments.

"You made us feel smart when we had to find the answers by ourselves, even though at the beginning it made us angry that you were only giving us hints," said Gabriel.

"I've always had the idea that a person achieves success because of luck. I realize that it isn't that way. If we want to succeed in life, it is worth taking risks. You gave us these tools. It is up to us to use them. What we are certain of is that if we use them, our path will be easier and safer. I discovered that **SUCCEEDING...IS AN ADVENTURE!**" says George.

Miss Patty smiles with satisfaction; her **AMBITIOUS TARGET** has been accomplished.

In this story, we have mentioned Anna as part of the group. We would like to honor her. She is an exceptional Mexican girl who has been a part of our lives and the lives of many other people. Her will to live made her accomplish high goals, even though she had limitations. She gave us an example of generosity, companionship, contagious joy, tenacity, and profound maturity, even though she was very young. She died in the year 2000, when she was 26-years-old, taking with her all her illusions and dreams of becoming a successful lawyer.

STUDY GUIDE

Do you experience conflicts with your parents? With your peers? Teachers? Boyfriend or girlfriend? Do you experience internal conflicts? Would you like to achieve your personal objectives? Would you like to be able to predict the potential consequences of your or someone else's actions? If you answer "yes" to any of these questions, you should give yourself the opportunity to learn the tools explained in this book.

These techniques, used in many countries and many settings, can help you improve your thinking skills and better yet, they are easy and fun!

If you think improving your thinking skill is important, say YES and start a new learning adventure that can help you succeed in life.

Section 1 RESOLVING CONFLICTS

The first tool we will learn is known as the cloud. The cloud allows us to have a better understanding of conflicts, to communicate them clearly, and to find solutions. Let's cover some basics first:

1. What is your definition of conflict?

   _____

   _____

   _____

2. Look for the meaning of the word CONFLICT and write it below.

   _____

   _____

   _____

3. Why are there conflicts between people?

_____

_____

_____

4. Do you think George has any conflicts? With whom?

_____

_____

_____

5. How does George react to a conflict?

_____

_____

_____

6. How did George's father react when George was insisting on going to the party?

_____

_____

_____

7. How do you think George felt when his father denied his request to go to the party?

_____

_____

_____

In the story, George follows various steps to solve his conflicts.

A) Briefly describe George's conflict with his father.

_____

_____

B) Identify WANTS

What does George want? Write it in the top box.   What does George's father want? Write it in the bottom box. The broken arrow between George's WANTS and his father's WANTS represents that they are in conflict.

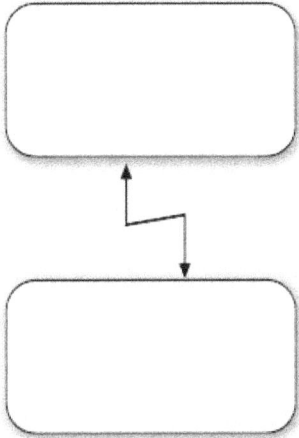

C) NEEDS

When a person is in a conflict and insists on having his/her WANT, it is because he/she is trying to fulfill a NEED.

Why do you think George wants to go to the party?

_____

_____

_____

Why do you think George's dad does not want him to go to the party?

_____

_____

_____

What is your definition of a need?

_____

_____

_____

List a few needs.

_____

_____

_____

"What is essential to every human being's development is considered a NEED" Example: I want to eat to **feed** myself, I want to sleep to **rest**, I want to go to the party to have **fun**, I want to study to **learn**.

Find the needs for the following examples:

I want to go to school to...

_____

_____

I want to go to the movie theater to...

_____

_____

I want to travel to…

_____

_____

George discovered that behind every WANT there is a NEED that has to be fulfilled.

Review the story and ask yourself why George wants to go to the party and write it in the corresponding square for his needs.

Now put yourself in George's father shoes and ask yourself what is the NEED he wants to fulfill by not letting George go to the party.

Write it in the corresponding square for George's dad need.

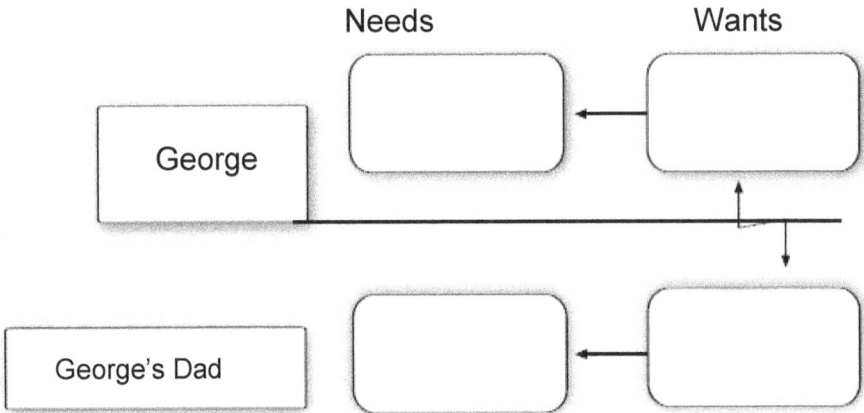

	Needs	Wants
George		
George's Dad		

D) COMMON OBJECTIVE

To complete the CLOUD CHART we need the last step, which is the COMMON OBJECTIVE.

Identifying this objective will help you find answers to the following questions.

Are both parties interested in solving the conflict? Why?

_____

_____

_____

What do you accomplish by fulfilling both NEEDS?

_____

_____

_____

Why does George want to fulfill his NEEDS with his father's consent?

_____

_____

_____

If this conflict would not have been solved, what would have been at risk?

_____

_____

_____

Do you think there is a common objective between George and his father?

Write it down in the following diagram.

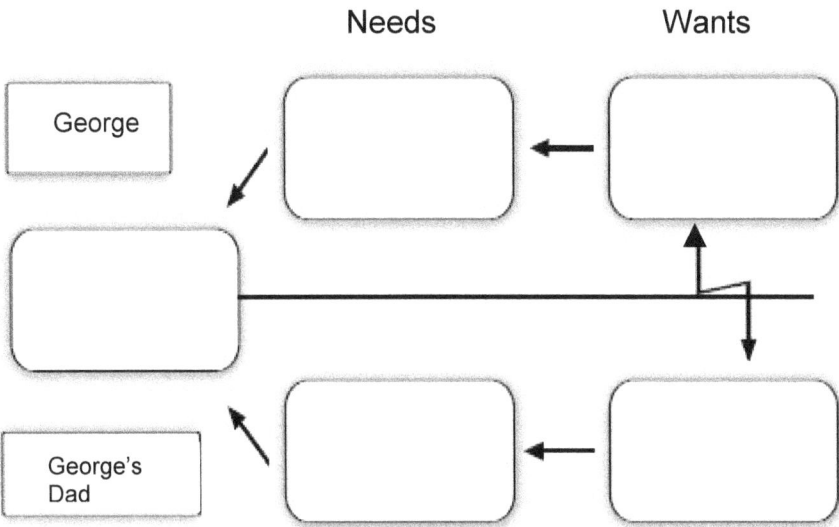

Needs | Wants

George

George's Dad

Notice that you built the CLOUD from right to left, starting with the WANTS in conflict and ending with the COMMON OBJECTIVE. Now, check to see if the CLOUD has logical meaning.

Read from left to right using the following steps. To facilitate communication, we have assigned a letter to each box as shown in the following diagram.

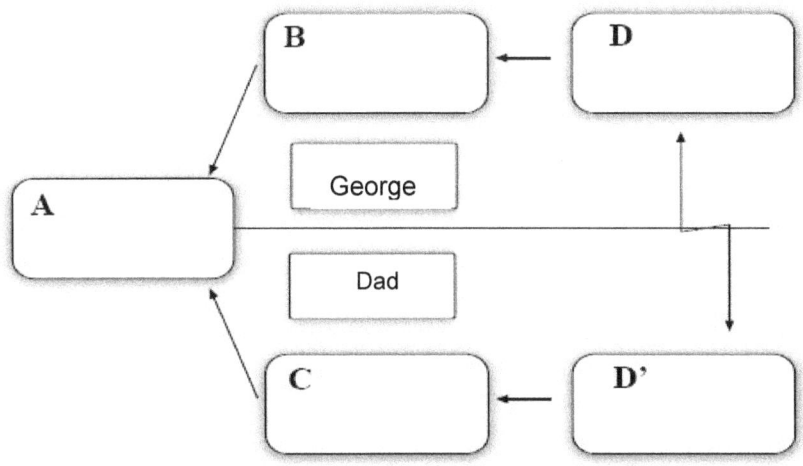

In order to do (A) -------------------- I must do (B) ------------------
                    Objective   *Need B*

In order to do (B) -------------------- I must do (D) ------------------
                    Need B   *Want D*

On the other hand:

In order to do (A) -------------------- I must do (C) ------------------
                    Objective   *Need C*

In order to do (C) -------------------- I must do (D') ------------------
                    Need C   *Want D'*

Does the reading of the cloud make sense to you? If not, modify it.

It is now time to start searching for a solution to the conflict. A good solution will allow BOTH people to satisfy their needs. We will call that a win-win solution.

Sometimes identifying the problem allows us to find a solution. Nevertheless, there are cases in which we require a deeper analysis. This is why the cloud gives us the opportunity to lay the foundation to find a solution by stating our assumptions.

E) ASSUMPTIONS

Why does George say that to "not disappoint Lucy," he "must" go to the party?

ASSUMPTIONS (B/D)
1._____
2._____
3._____

Why does George's father say that by not going to that party, George can improve his grades?
ASSUMPTIONS (C/D')
1._____
2._____
3._____

These arguments and explanations are called **ASSUMPTIONS**.

Observe that the <u>assumptions</u> explain why we insist that the only way of fulfilling a <u>need</u> is with that particular <u>want.</u>

Check that the <u>assumptions</u> on both sides justify the <u>want</u> with the <u>need.</u>

Assumptions are the seeds to finding solutions. If you can do something to make them invalid, then you have a potential solution. For example, an assumption could be "I cannot learn math." Is this valid? Maybe finding a tutor could prove this wrong. That is a potential solution.

Try to find assumptions and solutions for George's problem.

Assumption	Solution

We call ASSUMPTION INVALIDATION the process you just did.

F) WIN- WIN SOLUTIONS

A good solution—referred to as **INJECTION**—is one that fulfills the needs of both parties in the conflict.

What do you think is a good Injection for George's problem with his dad?

_____

_____

_____

Do you think it is **a win-win solution**? Why?

_____

_____

_____

To guarantee that the injection that you proposed is best, we suggest you analyze the pros and cons.

PROS AND CONS:

Analyze the pros and cons of your injection.

PROS	CONS

Try to see if the pros outweigh the cons, or try to find a way to eliminate (or reduce) the impact of the cons.

PRACTICE!

Now, we invite you to practice the cloud with a personal conflict. Remember that it is necessary that you be a part of the conflict.

1) Briefly describe the situation in which you find yourself in conflict.

_____

_____

_____

2) Identify wants.

Wants

My side

The other side

3) Identify each need.

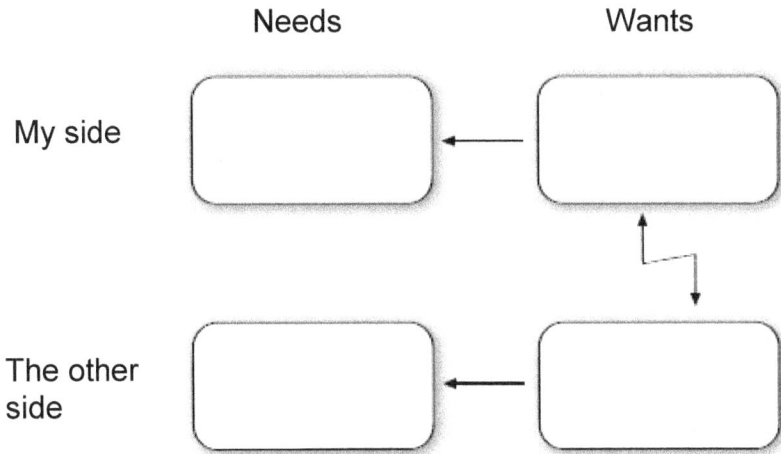

Needs   Wants

My side

The other side

4) Find the common objective.

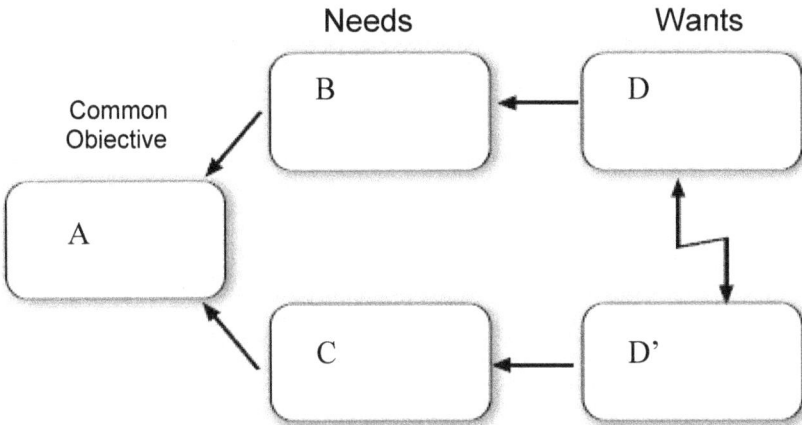

Needs   Wants

Common Obiective

B   D

A

C   D'

5) Find the assumptions.

BD

_____

_____

_____

CD'

_____

_____

_____

6)   Now you can invalidate them.

_____   _____

_____   _____

_____   _____

_____   _____

_____   _____

7)   Find the Injection that satisfies both needs, achieving a win-win solution.

_____

_____

_____

8)   Analyze the pros and cons of your Injection.

Pros   **Cons**

Consider that just one CON can weigh more than all the PROS.

Sometimes the struggles in which we find ourselves every day are with issues that are inside us. Peace begins in every human being's minds and hearts. When this happens, we begin to comprehend ourselves and others. When we realize that what is really important is to fulfill both needs, we will not be against each other, but together against the problem. Now, we have found a way to start a dialogue and solve conflicts.

Communicating with the cloud

You are experiencing a conflict with another person. When talking to that person, how should you communicate the conflict with them?

_____

_____

_____

Answer the following questions:

Should you start talking about the common objective, the needs or the wants?

_____

_____

_____

Whose needs and wants do you mention first? Why?

_____

_____

_____

Should you suggest a solution or should you wait for the other person to suggest it? Why?

_____

_____

_____

Congratulations! You have now a new tool to find win-win solutions to conflicts.

GLOSSARY

CLOUD: Logical diagram that describes a conflict situation.

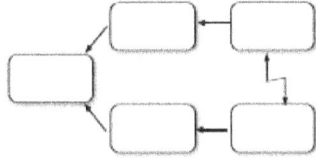

CONFLICT: A conflict between two persons occurs when the two persons' WANTS cannot co-exist. The conflict is presented in the CLOUD with a broken arrow.

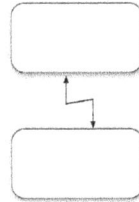

NECESSARY CONNECTING ARROW: This is read "To have this (head of the arrow) I must have (tail of the arrow)." These are logical connections that form the CLOUD. They exist between the WANTS, the NEEDS and the COMMON OJECTIVE.

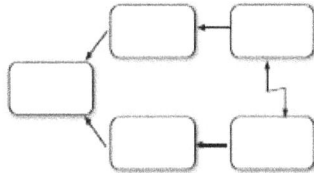

ASSUMPTIONS: Are explanations connections. The ASSUMPTIONS arrows BD and CD' are the base to claim why the WANTS are necessary to fulfill the NEEDS.

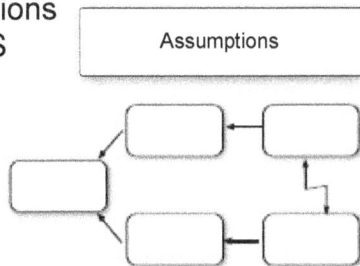

INJECTION: It is an alternative way to fulfill one NEED without hurting the other NEED.

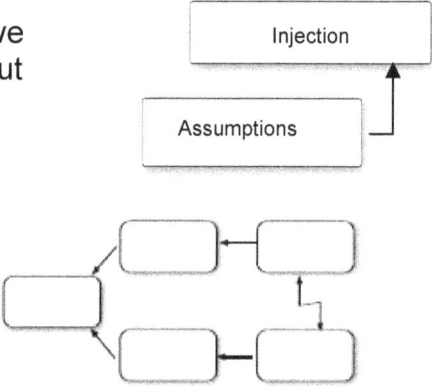

Section 2 ACHIEVING AMBITIOUS GOALS

Sometimes, we do not even try to reach our ambitious goals, because they look overwhelming. We do not even know where to start.

Why do you think that some goals seem so difficult to achieve?

_____

_____

_____

What is a good way to solve difficult problems?

_____

_____

In this section, we will learn about a tool called the ambitious target tool (AT). The AT allows you to breakdown a goal into smaller intermediate objectives, which then are ordered as steps in a ladder to reach your goals.

To breakdown the problem into smaller subproblems, we will take advantage of our intuition telling us how tough it is to reach the objective. Our brain is already feeling that there are a lot of obstacles blocking the way towards the goal. Let's revise the process that Miss Patty followed with the class trying to win the free trip.

1. Identify the ambitious target that the group chose and write it down in the box below. Notice how in the story, the group went through several versions of the ambitious target until a consensus was reached. It is important that you (or the team) are very clear about the target.

2. What were the **obstacles** students had to overcome to reach the goal of having the best average? Write them in the obstacles column in the next diagram. Obstacles block us from achieving our goals, but they can also serve as a guide to know what needs to be done in order to get closer to our goal.

3. For each obstacle, write an **intermediate objective** (IO). IO's are a way to overcome each obstacle. For example, if an obstacle you have is "I do not understand math," then potential Intermediate Objectives are "I find a tutor," "I talk to my teacher" or "I create a study group." Continuing with the book example, write the IO in the corresponding column after the obstacle.

OBSTACLE	IO

4. To build the ladder, you need to sequence the intermediate objectives. To facilitate the construction of the tool we suggest writing down each IO on a separate piece of paper.

Now as if you are doing a puzzle, arrange IOs (see next figure for an example of how the final tree may look) in the order you plan to tackle them, starting from the bottom and building up. Remember to take into account that each IO is necessary to advance to the next one and so on until you reach the ambitious target. The reason you need to sequence may be that the output of one IO is needed to start the next one. For example, "complete an internet search" may be needed before "gather notes from research sources." Also, remember that some IOs can be done parallel with other IOs, meaning that the output of one is not needed as an input for another one. This way, you can have multiple friends doing things at the same time, which can save you time.

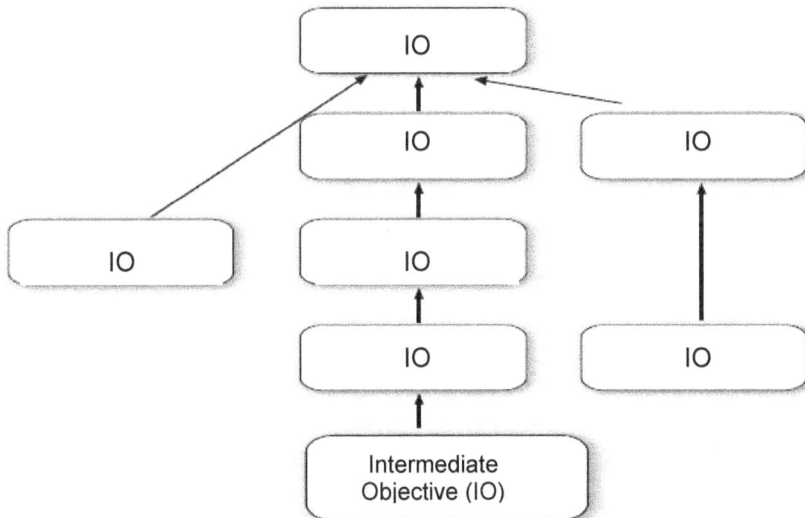

To check for the logical construction of your **tree,** we invite you to read it from top to bottom in the following way:

To reach the ambitious goal I should have achieved (previous IO)…and subsequently until you get to the root of the tree.

NOTE: It is important to remember that writing each IO on a separate piece of paper will help you move and shuffle them around until you are satisfied with the sequencing. Once you have the final tree constructed, you can use it as a blueprint and complete each IO, starting from the bottom and keeping at it until you are done. Without even knowing, you will achieve important ambitious goals in your life! You can use the AT to plan many things. Examples include writing a paper, planning a party, organizing your room, and winning a sports event. You can even use it when working in a group as it was done in the book. Remember, every time you feel you want to accomplish a goal but it seems overwhelming, use this tool!

Practice

Choose an ambitious personal goal and follow the steps to build the tree.

AMBITIOUS TARGET

OBSTACLES	INTERMEDIATE OBJECTIVES

GLOSSARY

AMBITIOUS GOAL:
An ambitious goal is a goal that seems unreachable, it needs a lot of effort to achieve.

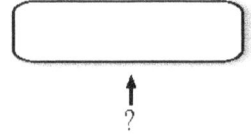

OBSTACLES:
An obstacle is something that does not allow us to reach an ambitious goal.
It is a problem we have to solve to reach our ambitious goal.

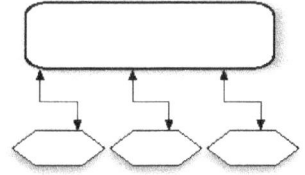

INTERMEDIATE OBJECTIVE:
An intermediate objective is a situation that makes the obstacle disappear when done. The intermediate objectives are the little goals I have to achieve to reach the ambitious goal.

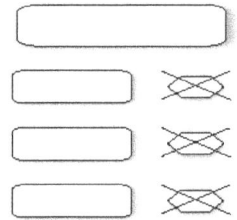

PREREQUISITE ARROW:
It indicates that the IO below must be completed first before the IO above.

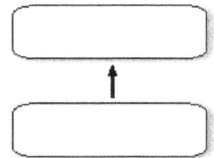

AMBITIOUS TARGET TREE:
It is a series of intermediate objectives representing the sequence of implementation.

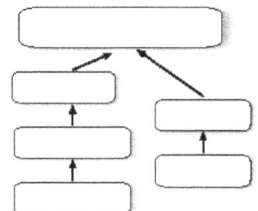

Section 3 THINKING LOGICALLY

Many of the things happening to us now are the result of the actions taken in the past. We took some of those actions without considering the long-term implications. As a result, in some cases, we were in trouble, and, in some cases, we did well. This may be because it is difficult to see the "long term," and we can only see the immediate effects of our actions. Wouldn't it be great if we had a tool that would help us predict what could happen in the future?

In this section, we will learn a new tool called The Logic Branch, which allows you to visualize the potential long-term consequences of your decisions. As a result, you can consider the positive or negative effects of your actions and make sound decisions.

The basic structure of The Logic Branch is presented in the next figure. Every decision, action or behavior results in an immediate effect because of a "reason." For example, if I let go of my pencil, then it will fall, because gravity exists. The initial action was letting the pencil go, the effect was the pencil falling, and the reason is gravity. Many times the effects do not stop there; the initial effect could become a cause for another effect because of another reason and so on. Continuing this process creates a chain of events until you reach a situation that is either good or bad.

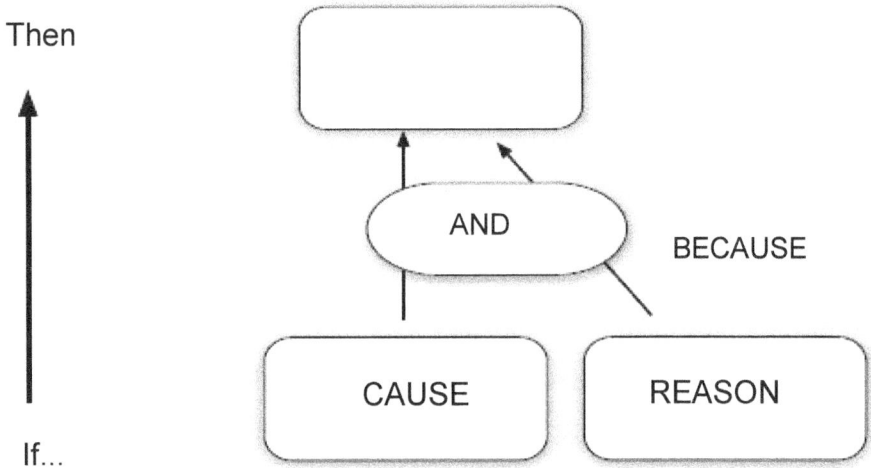

Then

If...

AND

BECAUSE

CAUSE

REASON

In the story, as you remember, the Zafiro gang challenged George's friends to fight outside of a bar on Saturday night. This caused a discussion between George's friends, because not all of them wanted to fight.

Miss Patty relied on the logic branch to guide her students to analyze the consequences of accepting the challenge or not.

Write down in the bottom square of the next diagram "WE ACCEPT THE CHALLENGE," and in the upper square, the immediate effect of accepting the challenge and the reason. Make sure that in each box you have complete sentences and that they are clear. After you are done writing, check to see if it makes sense by reading the branch this way: IF "the cause," THEN "the effect" BECAUSE "the reason." You will notice that the CAUSE and the REASON are united by an ellipse; this means that the CAUSE cannot produce that EFFECT by its own, and that on some occasions one or more REASONS are needed for that EFFECT to happen. If you do not know the reason, a little research may be necessary. You can ask your teacher, advisor and/or parents to help.

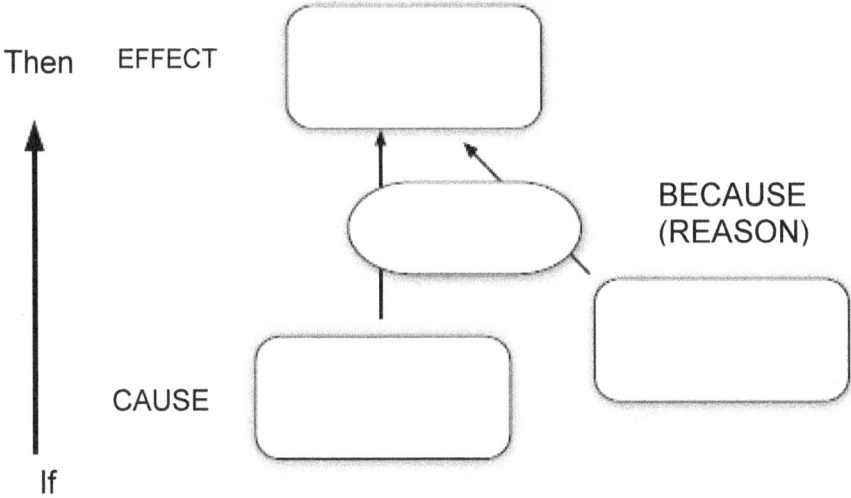

Then   EFFECT

CAUSE

If

BECAUSE
(REASON)

Using the diagram on the next page, continue building the branch until you come to an effect that gives you enough information to make a sound decision. This could be a very negative effect or a very positive effect. When the final effect is negative, The Logic Branch is referred to as a NEGATIVE BRANCH.

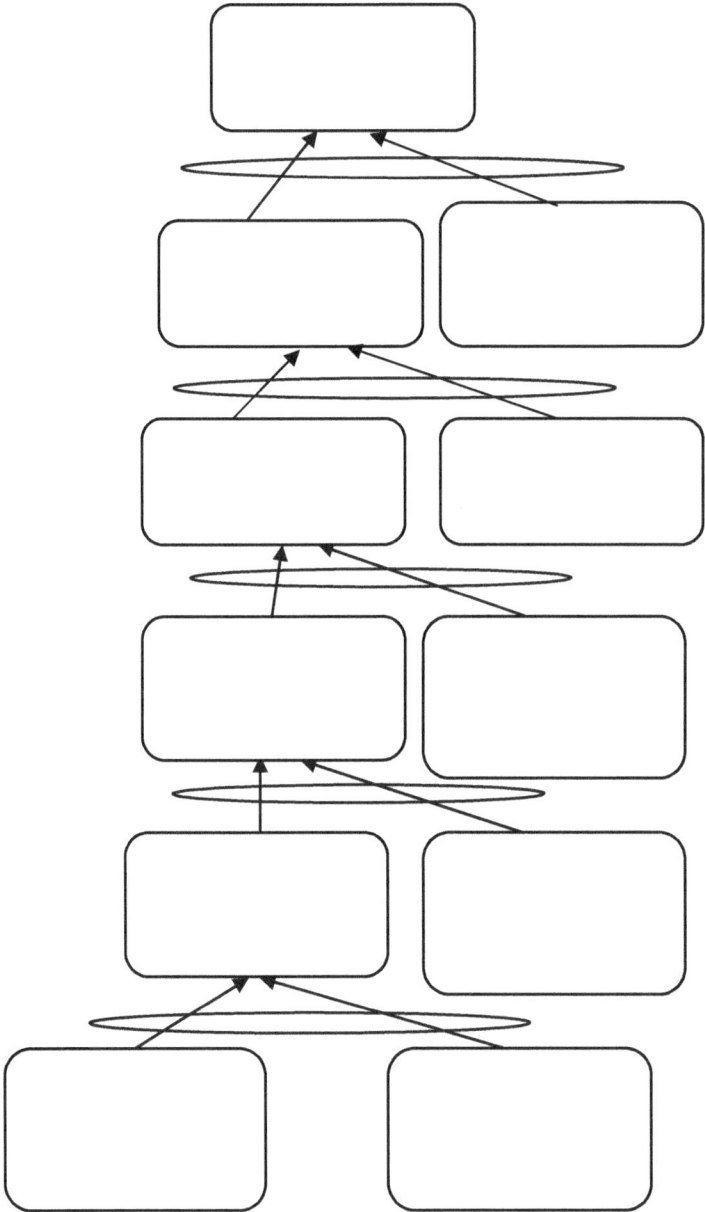

Let's assume your initial action leads you to a negative effect. What can you do? One thing you can do is simply not to take the actions, especially if intuitively you know it is a bad action. However, how about if your action is a good one, leading to a positive effect, but it can also result in a negative effect? For example, if an action is to study hard, this could lead you in the long term to be a successful person, but one negative may be that you miss the fun playing with your friends. In this example, why do you think you will not have time to play with your friends?

_____

_____

_____

What action can you take to avoid the negative effect?

_____

_____

_____

What you just did is called TRIMMING The Logic Branch. By finding an additional action that stops the chain of cause and effect, you prevent the negative from happening. So, The Logic Branch allows you not only to see the long-term consequences of your actions but also to generate actions that prevent negative effects. Isn't that something?

PRACTICE

Using the logic branch on the next page, find an initial action you are thinking about taking and analyze the long-term consequences of your action.

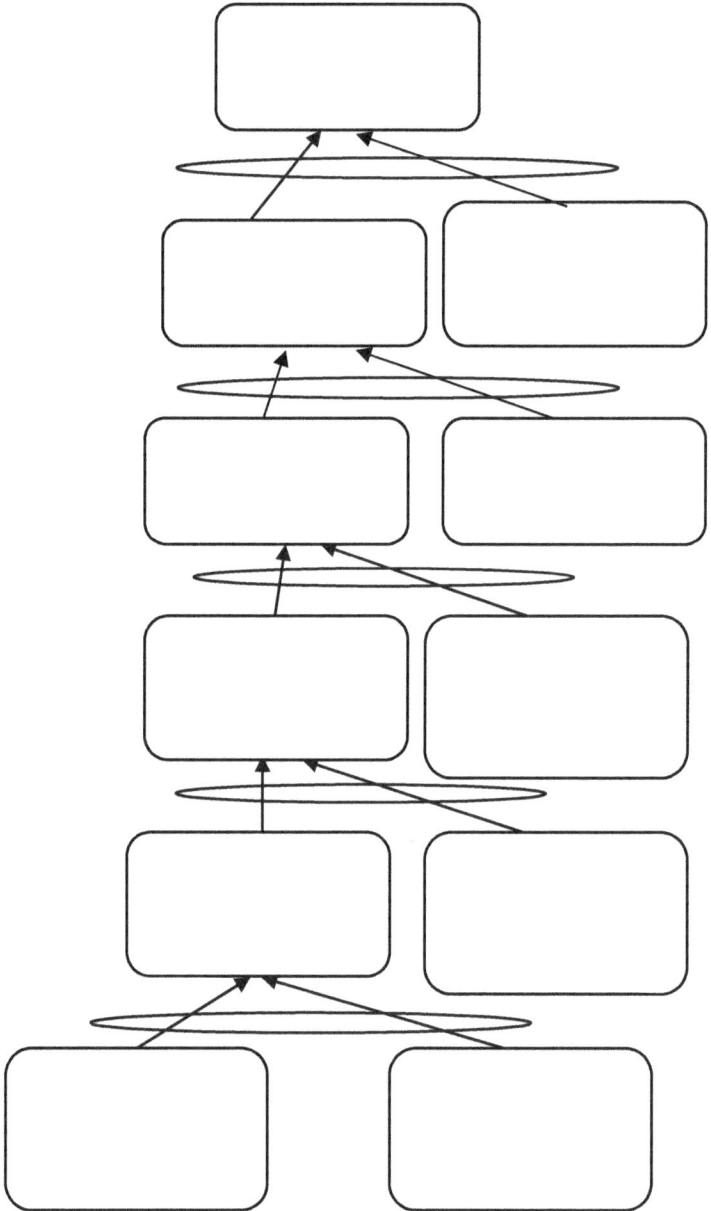

GLOSSARY

REASON: The reason (also referred to as an assumption) in The Logic Branch is the explanation for why we claim that the cause leads to the effect. The reasons are combined with the cause by an ellipse to symbolize that both have to exist in order for the effect to occur.

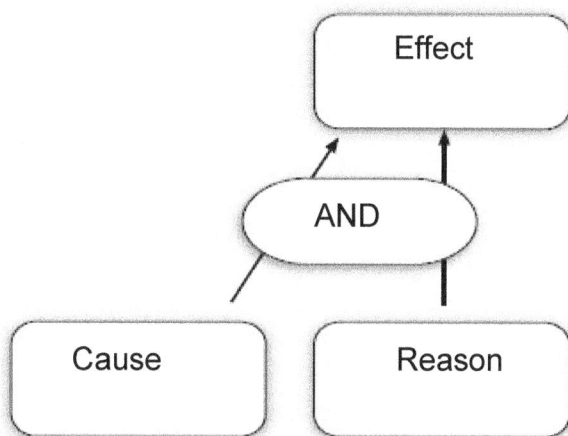

TRIMMING THE BRANCH: Finding an action that stops the chain of cause and effect sequences in a logic branch.

NEGATIVE BRANCH: It is a special case of The Logic Branch that describes the negative effect of carrying out certain ideas or behaviors.

FINAL QUESTIONS

What valuable knowledge did the students in the story acquire by using the tools?

What special skills did the students develop in this story?

_____

_____

_____

CONGRATULATIONS!!! Now you have in your hands a few tools that will go with you in your life journey. Because life is an adventure... failure or success depends on you. Remember, you have the FREEDOM to choose.

ADDITIONAL EXERCISES

Try to find and build more clouds from the different situations presented in the book.

While watching a movie or TV program, try to identify conflicts, assumptions, and solutions embedded in the story.

In the book, can you think of other ambitious targets students needed to achieve individually to improve the class average?

Construct an ambitious target tree for a project you have to do in class.

Write a logic branch, starting with the following entity: "I only eat junk food."

Write a logic branch for one of the topics from your classes (science, social studies, English, etc.).

www.ingramcontent.com/pod-product-compliance
Lightning Source LLC
Chambersburg PA
CBHW031001090426
42737CB00008B/624